CHILDREN'S FAVORITE ACTIVITY SONGS

Grey Squirrel

The Child's World®

Published in the United States of America by The Child's World®
1980 Lookout Drive • Mankato, MN 56003-1705
800-599-READ • www.childsworld.com

Acknowledgments
The Child's World®: Mary Berendes, Publishing Director
Editorial Directions: E. Russell Primm, Editor; Lucia Raatma, Proofreader
The Design Lab: Kathleen Petelinsek, Art Direction and Design;
   Anna Petelinsek and Victoria Stanley, Page Production

Library of Congress Cataloging-in-Publication Data
Grey squirrel / illustrated by Laura Ferraro Close.
     p. cm. — (Children's favorite activity songs)
  ISBN 978-1-60253-189-5 (library bound : alk. paper)
  1. Finger play. 2. Nursery rhymes. I. Ferraro Close, Laura, ill.
II. Title. III. Series.
  GV1218.F5G74 2009
  793—dc22   2009001571

ILLUSTRATED BY LAURA FERRARO CLOSE

Grey squirrel, grey squirrel!
Swish your bushy tail!

Grey squirrel, grey squirrel!
Swish your bushy tail!

Put a nut between your toes!

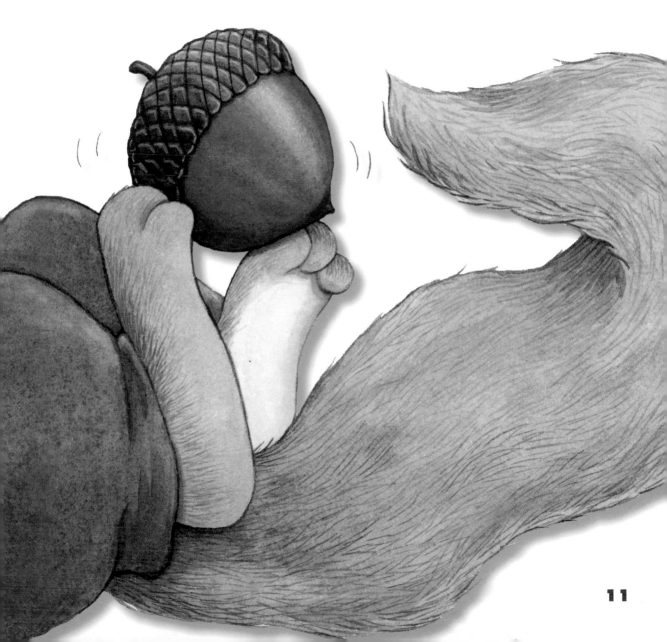

Grey squirrel, grey squirrel!
Swish your bushy tail!

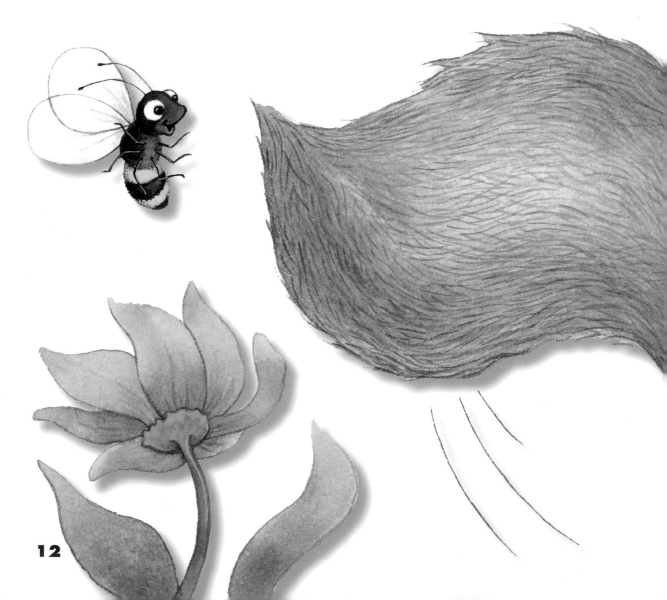

13

SONG ACTIVITY

Bounce up and down in rhythm when you say:
Grey squirrel, grey squirrel!

Pretend to shake your tail when you say:
Swish your bushy tail!

Poke your nose when you say:
Wrinkle up your little nose!

Touch your toes when you say:
Put a nut between your toes!

Bounce up and down in rhythm when you say:
Grey squirrel, grey squirrel!

Pretend to shake your tail when you say:
Swish your bushy tail!

BENEFITS OF NURSERY RHYMES AND ACTIVITY SONGS

Activity songs and nursery rhymes are more than just a fun way to pass the time. They are a rich source of intellectual, emotional, and physical development for a young child. Here are some of their benefits:

* Learning the words and activities builds the child's self-confidence—"I can do it all by myself!"

* The repetitious movements build coordination and motor skills.

* The close physical interaction between adult and child reinforces both physical and emotional bonding.

* In a context of "fun," the child learns the art of listening in order to learn.

* Learning the words expands the child's vocabulary. He or she learns the names of objects and actions that are both familiar and new.

* Repeating the words helps develop the child's memory.

* Learning the words is an important step toward learning to read.

* Reciting the words gives the child a grasp of English grammar and how it works. This enhances the development of language skills.

* The rhythms and rhyming patterns sharpen listening skills and teach the child how poetry works. Eventually the child learns to put together his or her own simple rhyming words— "I made a poem!"

ABOUT THE ILLUSTRATOR

Laura Ferraro Close got her start as an illustrator twenty-five years ago, working as a greeting card artist for a card company in Kansas City, Missouri. Today, Laura lives near Boston with her husband, two sons, a sweet dog, and two guinea pigs. Just outside their door is a forest where she can see lots of grey squirrels—but none that wear orange sweaters!